BOOK 1

Alfred's Music Tech Series

Composing Music With Notation

Floyd Richmond
Tom Rudolph
Lee Whitmore
Stefani Langol

©2007 Alfred Publishing Co., Inc.
16320 Roscoe Blvd., Suite 100
P.O. Box 10003
Van Nuys, CA 91410–0003

All Rights Reserved. Printed in USA.

ISBN-10: 0-7390-4075-8
ISBN-13: 978-0-7390-4075-1

Table of Contents

Alfred's Music Tech Series: Composing Music with Notation is designed for music students, grades 4–12, working together in a computer lab or individually. This book, or the accompanying teacher's manual (sold separately), may also be used successfully on the collegiate level by students studying elementary and secondary methods and by practicing music teachers who are taking graduate or continuing education courses in music technology. Upon completion of this book, students will have a broad understanding of the elements of music and the operation of notation software. Pre-service and in-service teachers will understand how to integrate notation software into the teaching of music. While an electronic instrument attached to the computer via MIDI would be useful, it is not required. *Alfred's Music Tech Series: Composing Music with Notation* is part of a larger series of books for use in a computer or keyboard lab. The series currently includes additional books on music production and electronic keyboard instruments.

■ Why read music notation?

Trained musicians, composers, and songwriters have written music so they can remember it later, can develop it further, and can share its performance with others. By learning to read musical notation, performers can experience a vast collection of written music. The masterpieces of the best composers through the ages have been written and preserved for our enjoyment. That music, while available to everyone through recordings, offers a much more complete and rewarding experience to those who can read and understand the symbols of music notation.

■ What does music notation tell the performer?

Anyone who listens to music knows that it is a complex system with many elements. The *melodies* that we sing or whistle remain in our memory. The *rhythms* to which we tap our feet give the music a sense of motion and energy. The *harmonies* produced as voices sing together to thicken the texture and add a sense of tension and resolution to the music. The *form* (structure) of the music becomes evident as we listen to repeating and contrasting sections. The *expression* of emotion in music stimulates us as the tempos and styles of music change. Music notation describes each of these aspects in enough detail that a performer can play it as intended by the composer.

■ What's so great about music notation software?

Currently available notation programs enable those who use them to enter notes into the computer by clicking the mouse or by playing an instrument, to listen to the notes entered, to correct mistakes, and to print professional-quality copies. Music may also be scanned into the computer, posted to the web, or integrated into word-processing programs, presentation software, or home movies.

■ What notation software should I use?

This book is designed for use with any modern notation program. Users of Finale® and Sibelius® will find files in an appropriate format on the accompanying CD. Users of other notation programs may import standard MIDI files from the CD into their software to complete the activities. A fully functional copy of one of these programs would be very useful to the reader, but many of the activities can be completed with demonstration versions of the software. Demonstration versions of Finale and Finale NotePad® are available online at http://www.makemusic.com. A demonstration version of Sibelius is available from http://www.sibelius.com.

■ What's in this book?

This introduction will tell you about the book. Units 1–5 help students learn to use music notation software, to understand music, and to write music of their own. The Appendix explains the fundamentals of music and rules of notation.

■ What's on the CD?

The accompanying data CD is designed for use with a computer. To begin, students open the folder for their notation program: Finale, Sibelius, MIDI (for other notation programs), and SmartMusic® (for supplemental activities). Inside each of these folders, are materials to be used with each unit of the book. For example, when the student is working on "Activity 1.1" in the book, they would open the file called "Unit 1.1" on the CD and complete the activity found there. Assuming the student has Finale or Sibelius installed on their computer, they need only to double-click a file to open it. Occasionally, an MP3 or other media file will be encountered. These are for listening activities in the book. When double-clicked, they should open and play in an appropriate media player.

■ What's in the Teacher's Manual?

General instructions for completing each activity are found throughout this book. Additional instructions are found in the teacher's manual (sold separately). The scope of this book does not permit a comprehensive explanation of all concepts. The teacher's manual contains more information on the implementation of each lesson. This book contains suggestions for supplemental study within every lesson. The teacher's manual includes additional supplemental materials and tips for using them. The teacher's manual is also designed to assist in the process of curriculum development and daily lesson planning.

■ Conclusion

The goals of this book are to:

- Teach or review the basic symbols of written notation.
- Introduce the student to the use of notation software.
- Give readers a greater understanding of music.
- Encourage musical thinking and composition.

Students will complete projects that will expose them to a variety of musical concepts. They will listen to, analyze, reconstruct, improvise, arrange, and compose music in every lesson. They will learn to think musically. The use of notation software makes advanced musical concepts assessable to a wider and younger audience and in an approachable way that would not be possible in the traditional music classroom.

Floyd Richmond

Tom Rudolph

Lee Whitmore

Stefani Langol

Conventions Used In This Book

 This icon indicates that there is a supporting file on the accompanying CD. These files contain either listening examples or notation activities. When you view the CD, you'll find that the files are organized into folders corresponding to the units in the book and that the files in each folder are listed in order of appearance in the book.

 This icon represents a good point in the lesson to save your work. Of course, saving more frequently is recommended.

Entering a Song (Notation, Lyrics, Expressions)

■ Objectives

Upon completion of this unit, you will be able to do the following:

- Create a new song.
- Enter notes.
- Play the song and parts of the song.
- Add lyrics and titles (words).
- Copy and paste music from one location to another.
- Add expressive markings such as tempo and dynamic changes.

- Change instruments.
- Create a three-voice performance of a round.
- Insert dynamic markings musically.
- Insert tempo markings musically.
- Orchestrate a three-voice round.

■ Activity 1.1 Entering a Song by Hand

Using a pencil, copy the notes into the empty measures. Be certain to make the copy look as much like the original as possible.

- Noteheads should be notated clearly on a line or space.
- Stems should be drawn the same length and direction as the originals.
- Stems should be drawn from the appropriate side of the note head.
- Draw neatly!

Are You Sleeping?

French Folk Tune

Are You Sleeping?

French Folk Tune

■ Activity 1.2 Entering a Song into the Computer

 From the companion data CD, open the file Unit01-01 ("Are You Sleeping?") in your notation program and play the song. Compare the notation on screen to your hand-written copy. Which is neater?

Now enter "Are You Sleeping?" using your notation software

1. Launch your notation program or create a new blank document by choosing NEW from the FILE menu.

2. Follow the instructions on screen. Most notation programs use a setup assistant that asks a series of questions about the music.

3. The title is "Are You Sleeping?"

4. The composer is "French Folk Tune."

5. The song will need a single staff, preferably with a piano sound.

6. The key signature is C major.

7. The time signature is 4/4.

8. The piece does not use pickup notes.

9. After entering the notes, your song should look like the one below.

YOU MAY NEED TO KNOW

The process for entering notes in most notation programs is as follows:

1. Select the desired note (eighth, quarter, half).

2. Point and click at the correct location on the staff (on the exact line or space).

3. Repeat this process until all notes have been entered.

4. If a mistake is made, an easy way to correct it is to immediately go to the EDIT menu and choose UNDO. On most computers, typing ⌘-Z (Mac) or CTRL-Z (Windows) will also undo the last operation.

The notes used in "Are You Sleeping?"	
	Half Notes
	Quarter Notes
	Eighth Notes (Written in groups)
	Eighth Notes (Written individually) *May appear temporarily.*

Are You Sleeping?

French Folk Tune

Saving the Song

With all computer programs, it is important to frequently save your work. The disk icon will be used throughout the text as a reminder. From the FILE menu, choose SAVE. The computer will ask for the following:

1.   The title of the piece (Are You Sleeping?)

2.   The format (the default format of the notation program is best)

3.   The location where the file is to be saved

Typically, the file will be saved into the computer's documents folder, although circumstances may require saving it to another location, such as on a CD or network drive. Regardless, it is important to remember the name of the song and where it is being saved so it can be found for use in the future.

The next time you save this song, you won't see these questions again. The computer remembers the answers!

Playing the Song

Press play to listen to the piece. Generally, notation software has standard play controls as shown below, but if they are not visible, a play option is usually available in one of the windows or menus. In order to play a part of the song, indicate a starting measure (either by selecting it or typing its number before pressing play).

Play Controls

| Move to Beginning | Rewind | Record | Play | Pause | Stop | Fast Forward | Move to End |

■ Activity 1.3 Entering Lyrics

Up to this point, the notation has been designed for piano players or instrumentalists, but those who sing would appreciate the words (lyrics). Using the lyric capabilities of the notation program, enter the lyrics shown below.

1. Tell the notation program to enter lyrics (select the lyric option from the appropriate menu).

2. Click the first note where the lyrics are to appear.

3. Type the words into the song using a space between words, and hyphens between syllables such as sleep-ing, bro-ther, morn-ing, and ring-ing. The correct placement of hyphens is shown below.

> **Are you sleep-ing, Are you sleep-ing,**
>
> **Bro-ther John? Bro-ther John?**
>
> **Morn-ing bells are ring-ing,**
>
> **Morn-ing bells are ring-ing,**
>
> **Ding, Ding, Dong. Ding, Ding, Dong.**

When finished, the lyrics will appear in the song as shown below.

Are You Sleeping?

French Folk Tune

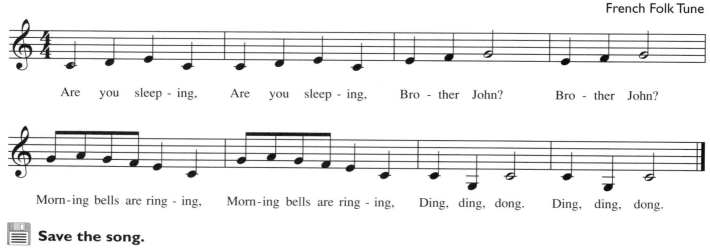

Save the song.

■ Putting Your Name on the Song

1. Choose the appropriate menu or tool to enter the text.

2. Type "Entered by [Your First and Last Name]" as indicated below.

3. Drag the text to the left as indicated below.

Save the song.

■ Printing the Song

From the FILE menu choose PRINT, then click OK.

■ Congratulations! You've finished your first song!

Create new lyrics for "Are You Sleeping?" An example is shown below.

Hump - ty Dump - ty, Hump - ty Dump - ty, On the wall, On the wall,

Now the wind is blow - ing, Now poor Hump - ty's fall - ing, Oh no, no. Oh no, no.

■ **Your Lyrics**

1. Enter new lyrics below the notes shown here. Be creative.
2. Open the file Unit01-01a and enter the new lyrics.
3. Print the new version of the song.
4. Ask someone to sing the new lyrics that you composed.

Are You Sleeping?

French Folk Tune

💾 **Save the song.**

■ Activity 1.5 Copying and Pasting

You've finished your first song, but now, we are going to learn a way to make entering the music faster and easier. This same technique will make it easier to compose later. The song, "Are You Sleeping?", uses many of the same measures over and over. Repetition is common in music. Instead of re-entering these measures each time, it is possible to copy them. This process is called "Copying and Pasting."

In the song below, the empty measures are to be filled with exactly the same notes and words as the previous measure. One way of doing this might be to photocopy the four measures written below, cut them, then paste them into the empty measures.

Fortunately for us, the computer provides an easy way to do this.

 1.   Open the file Unit01-02.

2.   The screen shown below will appear.

3.   Copy and paste each written measure into the measure following it using the notation software.

YOU MAY NEED TO KNOW

The process for copying and pasting in most programs is as follows:	The steps for copying and pasting music using your notation program:
1. Choose the selection tool if necessary.	*(Write here)*
2. Select the desired measure.	**Step 1:**
3. From the EDIT menu, choose COPY.	_____
4. Select the measure where the notes are to be placed.	**Step 2:**
5. Choose PASTE from the EDIT menu.	_____
6. Some programs provide shortcuts for this process, such as dragging and dropping the music in place, or ALT-clicking (Windows) or option-clicking (Mac) a measure where the selection is to be copied.	**Step 3:** _____

Are You Sleeping?

French Folk Tune

Are   you   sleep - ing,   Bro - ther   John?

Morn - ing bells are ring - ing,   Ding, ding, dong.

■ **Save the song.**

■ Rounds

Some songs are written so they may be played or sung as a round. These include songs such as "Row, Row, Row Your Boat," "Kookaburra," "Scotland's Burning," and "Are You Sleeping?" In a round, one group of singers or instruments starts singing or playing. In a measure or two, another group begins, but from the beginning. Because of the way the song is written, a pleasing harmony is produced. Frequently, additional groups may also join.

 1. Open the file <u>Unit01-03</u> and press play. A three-voice round based on the tune "Are you Sleeping?" will play.

2. Can you tell when each group enters?

■ Activity 1.6 Creating a Three-Part Round

Create a three-part round using the song "Are You Sleeping?"

 1. Open the file <u>Unit01-04</u>.

2. Using the skills learned in this chapter, copy and paste the music from staff one into staves two and three where indicated.

3. Play the file to be sure it is correct.

Notation programs permit more than one measure to be copied at a time: To select several measures at a time, click the first measure (or note), then shift-click the last. The finished song is shown below.

Are You Sleeping?

French Folk Tune

 Save the song.

■ Expressive Markings

Composers often try to make their music more interesting through the use of expressive markings. These include:

- **Dynamics:** how loud or soft the music is performed.

- **Tempo:** how fast or slow the music is performed.

- **Instrumentation:** which instruments are used.

In this section, the notation and entry of expressive markings will be covered. These markings will be added to the song to produce a better performance of "Are You Sleeping?"

■ Activity 1.7 Dynamics

Composers use dynamics (loudness and softness) to make their music more interesting.

Listen to the following example:

 1. Open the file <u>Unit01-05</u>.

2. Play the file.

How are the dynamics in the second part different from the first? Write your answer below.

_____

Adding Dynamic Markings to an Existing Song:

 1. Open the file <u>Unit01-06</u>.

2. Enter dynamic markings to make the piece more musical.

3. Use the dynamic markings indicated in the song below. (Set the beginning of the first measure to *mp*, the third to *mf*, the fifth to *f*, and the seventh to *mf*.)

Are You Sleeping?

French Folk Tune

■ Dynamics

Enter dynamic markings into the song as indicated below.

Adding Dynamic Markings to an Existing Song:

  1. Open the file Unit01-07.

2. Enter dynamic markings to make the piece more musical.

3. Use the dynamic markings indicated in the song below. (Set the beginning of the first entrance to *mp*, the second to *mf*, the third to *f*.)

Why do you think these dynamic markings help improve the music? *Hint:* Composers and performers frequently think about the balance and blend of parts as they compose and perform. Can you hear each entering part clearly without the dynamic markings? _____

_____

Are You Sleeping?

French Folk Tune

💾 **Save the song.**

■ Experiment with Dynamic Changes

Try setting the dynamics to other values. Perhaps it would be more effective to begin at a louder level (*mf*, *f*, then *ff*). Another possibility might be to increase the dynamics by more than one level at each entry. For instance, the first voice could be *p*, the second *mf*, and the third *ff*. Finally, it might help to set a different dynamic level as each voice finishes. The goal is to make the performance as pleasing as possible.

 Save the song.

YOU MAY NEED TO KNOW

Terms and abbreviations commonly used to indicate dynamic changes in music

Italian	Abbreviation	English
Fortissimo	*ff*	Very loud
Forte	*f*	Loud
Mezzo forte	*mf*	Moderately loud
Mezzo piano	*mp*	Moderately soft
Piano	*p*	Soft
Pianissimo	*pp*	Very soft

The steps for changing dynamics in a piece of music:

Generally, a tool or menu option (usually called expressions) permits dynamic markings to be entered into the song. The general process for entering dynamics (expressions) is indicated below.

1. Choose the tool or option for creating dynamics.
2. Click or double-click where the dynamics are to be inserted.

Some programs provide shortcuts for this process, such as dragging and dropping the music in place, or control-clicking or option-clicking a measure where the selection is to be copied.

The steps for changing dynamics using your notation program:

(Write here)

Step 1:

_____

Step 2:

_____

Step 3:

_____

Alfred's Music Tech Series

■ Activity 1.8 Gradual Dynamic Changes

The dynamic markings on the previous page refer to immediate changes in the volume of the music. As soon as the performer sees f, they begin to play loudly. Other dynamic markings, as indicated below, tell the performers to make gradual changes.

YOU MAY NEED TO KNOW

Terms and abbreviations commonly used to indicate gradual dynamic changes

Italian	Abbreviation	Symbol	English
Crescendo	**Cresc.**		Gradually get louder
Decrescendo	**Decresc.**		Gradually get softer

The process for entering crescendos and decrescendos in most programs:

1. Select the appropriate tool or mode (a crescendo or hairpin).
2. Click or double-click where the crescendo or decrescendo should start.
3. Indicate where the crescendo or decrescendo should stop. Usually this is done by dragging the mouse or tapping the space bar.

The steps for entering crescendos and decrescendos using your notation program:

(Write here)

Step 1:

_____

Step 2:

_____

Step 3:

_____

Apply the following dynamic markings to every two measures in the song below. Try other patterns as well.

💾 **Save the song.**

■ Activity 1.9 Tempo

Composers use tempo markings (the speed of the music) to set a mood or make the music more playable.

Listen to the following example:

 1. Open the file <u>Unit01-08</u>. (Unit 1-Tempo1)

2. Play the file.

How are the tempos in the second section different from the first?

YOU MAY NEED TO KNOW

Terms commonly used to indicate tempo changes in music:

Italian	English
Largo	Slow and broad
Adagio *or* Lento	Slow, but moving
Andante	Slow
Moderato	Moderate
Allegro	Quickly
Vivace	Fast
Presto	Very fast

The steps for changing tempo in a piece of music:

Generally, a tool, menu or text option permits tempo markings to be entered into the song.

1. Choose the tool or option for creating tempo markings.

2. Click or double-click where the tempo marking is to be inserted.

The steps for changing tempo using your notation program: *(Write here)*

Step 1:

_____

Step 2:

_____

Step 3:

_____

Adding Tempo Markings to an Existing Song

Composers and conductors consider a number of tempos before deciding which best communicates what they are trying to express and which works the best for their ensemble.

 1. Open the file <u>Unit01-09</u>.

2. Select a tempo marking appropriate for the piece.

3. Experiment with several fast and slow tempo markings and choose one appropriate for the piece.

Do some seem too slow, too fast? Do some tempo markings seem more reflective, more energetic?

Are You Sleeping?

Save the song.

■ Activity 1.10 Gradual Tempo Changes

The tempo markings on the previous page refer to immediate changes in the music. For example, as soon as performers see *andante*, they begin to play slowly. Other tempo markings (*accelerando* and *ritard*) tell the performers to make gradual changes as indicated below. Although for this piece, the most musical effect would be to place a *ritard* near the end. Experiment with each of these tempo changes to learn what they do.

 Save the song.

YOU MAY NEED TO KNOW

Terms and abbreviations commonly used to indicate gradual tempo changes:

Italian	Abbreviation	English
Accelerando	*Accel.*	Gradually faster
Ritard *or* Ritardando	*Rit.*	Gradually slower

The process for entering accelerando and ritard in most programs:

1. Select the appropriate tool or mode.

2. Click or double-click where the accelerando or ritard should start.

3. Indicate where the accelerando or ritard should stop.

NOTE: Some programs may require additional steps in order to observe these markings. Check your user manual for specific instructions.

The steps for entering accelerando and ritard using your notation program:

(Write here)

Step 1:

_____

Step 2:

_____

Step 3:

_____

■ Activity 1.11 Instrumentation Changes

As each part enters, the texture of "Are You Sleeping?" becomes thicker. By the third entry, it is difficult to hear each new melody. Although the appropriate use of dynamics helps, another option is to have a different instrument play each part.

1. Set the voice of each staff to a different instrument.
2. Experiment with different instruments on each voice.
3. Identify a combination that works well.
4. Play the piece for the class.

YOU MAY NEED TO KNOW

The process for changing instruments in most programs is as follows:

1. Display the notation program's "instrument list" or "mixer" window.

2. Select an instrument sound to play each staff.

The steps for changing instruments using your notation program:

(Write here)

Step 1:

_____

Step 2:

_____

Step 3:

_____

Are You Sleeping?

Andante

French Folk Tune

Save the song.

Enrichment Activities

1. Enter the lyrics for "Are You Sleeping?"—second verse in French.
    http://www.niehs.nih.gov/kids/lyrics/frere.htm

    > **Frè-re Jac-ques, Frè-re Jac-ques,**
    >
    > **Dor-mez vous? Dor-mez vous?**
    >
    > **Son-nez les ma-ti-nes, Son-nez les ma-ti-nes**
    >
    > **Ding, Ding, Dong. Ding, Ding, Dong.**

2. Compose a countermelody to "Are You Sleeping?" or accompaniment using whole and half notes. Stick to the notes C, E, and G. Be creative. Look for sounds that sustain.

3. Use the drum groove or rhythm-section generator to create an accompaniment to "Are You Sleeping?"

Web Extensions

On the CD companion disc, open the projects listed below.

 1. The melody of "Frère Jacques" was used by Mahler in the 2nd movement of his first symphony. Listen to a MIDI file. How did he change the melody? http://www.mfiles.co.uk/Scores/Mahler1-3ext.htm. A notation file containing part of the Mahler Symphony is included on the accompanying CD (Unit01-10 or Unit01-11). Open it in your notation program and listen as it is played.

2. Research information on the origin of this French folk song. http://www.google.com

3. List other songs that are rounds. For a list of additional rounds, see http://www.bussongs.com/round_songs.php.

4. Copy and paste the lyrics from a web site into a word-processing document. http://www.niehs.nih.gov/kids/search.htm

5. Go to a sheet music site such as http://www.mysheetmusic.com. Print out a piece that you like and enter it in your notation program.

Multimedia Extensions:

Create a PowerPoint or Keynote presentation and include the following information:

1. Define a round.

2. How is a round created?

3. Background on "Frère Jacques"

4. How to use expressive markings effectively

Computer-Assisted Instruction Software Extensions:

Lessons from *Music Ace I* Software (www.harmonicvision.com)

1. Lesson 12: Loud and Soft, Same Pitch

2. Lesson 16: Same Pitch, Different Timbres

Lessons from *Music Ace II*

3. Lesson 1: Beat and Tempo

4. Lesson 2: Hearing Rhythms

Lessons from *Alfred's Essentials of Music Theory*, Volume I (www.alfred.com)

1. Measure, Bar Line and Double Bar Line

2. Dynamic Signs, Tempo Marks and Articulation

SmartMusic practice activity. A copy of the SmartMusic files for "Frère Jacques," "London Bridge," and "Jingle Bells" are found on the accompanying data CD, in the SmartMusic folder.

1. Load the song(s) into SmartMusic.

2. Sing or play along.

Keyboard Connection

1. Perform "Are You Sleeping" on the piano keyboard.

Sequencing Connections

1. Create an arrangement of "Are You Sleeping." Choose timbres, select tempo, set volume and panning.

■ Notes

Arranging

Objectives

In this lesson, several notation and musical skills will be practiced:

- Copying and pasting music from one location to another.

- Identifying repeated and contrasting sections of music.

- Reconstructing familiar tunes from musical building blocks.

- Harmonizing a given melody with musical building blocks.

Repetition and Contrast

In Unit 1, "Are You Sleeping?" contained many repeated measures. While songs frequently do not contain as much, most do use some repetition. Repetition helps us remember and understand music. Composers include many parts that are the same and many that are different. Being able to remember and identify parts that are similar and different is a basic skill required for understanding and listening to music.

Activity 2.1 Rebuilding London Bridge

Listening

 A familiar childhood song is "London Bridge." Open the file Unit02-01 and play it. Can you identify parts that are repeated?

Reconstruction

In the activity below, five building blocks are given. These can be used to create the song "London Bridge." Copy and paste them to the correct locations in the blank measures below.

 1. Open the file Unit02-02.

2. Play each building block. Some measures may be used more than once. (Repetition)

3. Once you know the correct location of each building block, copy and paste it into the correct measure.

4. Print your music or write the correct answer by hand below.

London Bridge

English Folk Tune

 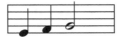  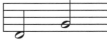

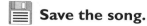

Experiment with different dynamics.

1. Choose a tempo.

2. Choose different instruments.

3. Compose and enter new lyrics.

4. Volunteer to play your new version for the class.

5. Create an original version of "London Bridge."

 Save the song.

Activity 2.2 Rebuilding Jingle Bells

Listening

Open the file Unit02-03, and play it. Can you identify the repeated parts?

Reconstruction

In the activity below, nine building blocks which can be used to create the song "Jingle Bells" are given. Copy and paste them to the correct locations in the blank measures below.

1. Open the file Unit02-04.

2. Play each building block.

3. Some measures may be used more than once.

4. Once you know the correct order of the building blocks, copy and paste each into the correct measure.

5. Print your music or write the correct patterns by hand below.

Jingle Bells

James Pierpoint

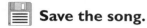

❏ Experiment with different dynamics.

❏ Choose a tempo.

❏ Choose different instruments. "Jingle Bells" includes an accompaniment in a second staff. Set the instrument of each staff.

❏ Compose and enter new lyrics.

❏ Volunteer to play your version for the class.

 Save the song.

■ Activity 2.3 More Building Blocks

The following piece, excerpted from a longer work by Mozart, allows composition using building blocks.

1. Open the file Unit02-05. You will see the music below. Play the file. You'll hear an accompaniment with no melody.

2. Build a melody in the top staff by copying and pasting from the measures directly below each empty measure.

3. Repeat this process until all empty measures have been filled. Don't copy music into any location except into the measures directly above.

4. Listen to your song. If you like it, save it. If not, replace the notes in the top staff with other choices.

5. When finished, play your version for the class. The score has been prepared so that only the top and bottom staves play.

Why do only the top and bottom staves play? Why do you suppose that you are required to select the melodies from those directly below each empty measure?

_____

_____

Minuet Builder

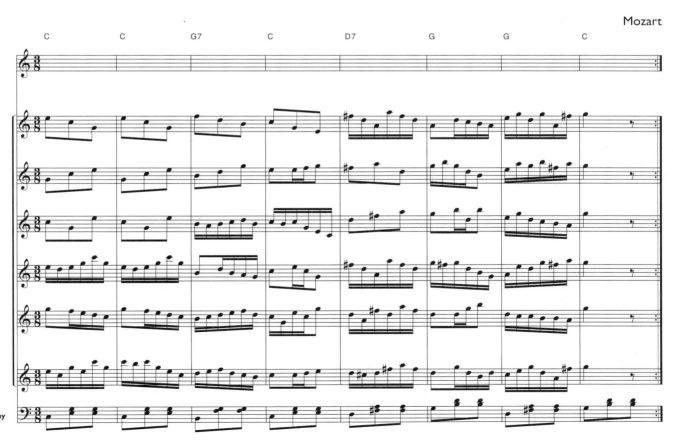

■ Additional Activities and Reflections

As long as you correctly follow the instructions on the previous page, you will build a pleasant piece. Even so, there may be some things that could make the piece better.

1. Are all of the rhythms selected fast? Slow? If mixed, are they mixed in a symmetrical pattern? (Alternating fast, slow; slow, fast, etc.?)_____

2. Do all of the contours move up? Down? If mixed, are they balanced or symmetrical? _____

3. Experiment with repeating and contrasting rhythms and contours for a more musical result.

■ Harmonize a Song

This song uses a single chord for its harmony. Numbers 1 through 4 below present this chord in rhythmic patterns that can be used to complete the empty measures. Choose a harmonic and rhythmic pattern and copy it into each of the empty measures below.

 1. Open the file Unit02-06.

2. Harmonize the song by copying and pasting the building blocks into the empty measures.

3. Try using various patterns.

4. Listen to your work and play it for a classmate.

YOU MAY NEED TO KNOW

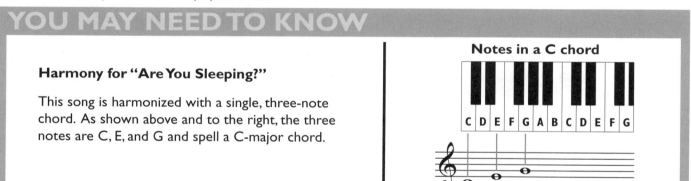

Harmony for "Are You Sleeping?"

This song is harmonized with a single, three-note chord. As shown above and to the right, the three notes are C, E, and G and spell a C-major chord.

Notes in a C chord

Are You Sleeping?

French Folk Tune

Are you sleep-ing, Are you sleep-ing, Bro-ther John? Bro-ther John?

Morn-ing bells are ring-ing, Morn-ing bells are ring-ing, Ding, ding, dong. Ding, ding, dong.

Save the song.

Alfred's Music Tech Series

■ Harmonize a Song with C and G Chords

Chord symbols are found in the music below to indicate where each chord should be placed. Above the song are chords in a rhythmic pattern which can be used to complete the empty measures. Copy and paste each of the accompaniment patterns into an appropriate empty measure.

 1. Open the file Unit02-07.

2. Harmonize the song below by copying and pasting the chord patterns at the top of the song into an appropriate empty measure.

3. Listen to your work.

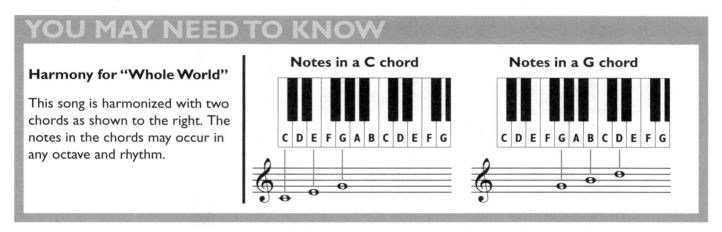

YOU MAY NEED TO KNOW

Harmony for "Whole World"

This song is harmonized with two chords as shown to the right. The notes in the chords may occur in any octave and rhythm.

Notes in a C chord

Notes in a G chord

He's Got the Whole World

 Save the song.

■ Harmonize a Song with C, F and G Chords

In the song below, chord symbols are found above the music. The chords at the top of the printout below are used to complete the empty measures. Copy each of the accompaniment patterns into an appropriate empty measure.

1. Open the file Unit02-08.

2. Harmonize the song by copying and pasting the building blocks with the correct harmony.

3. Listen to your work.

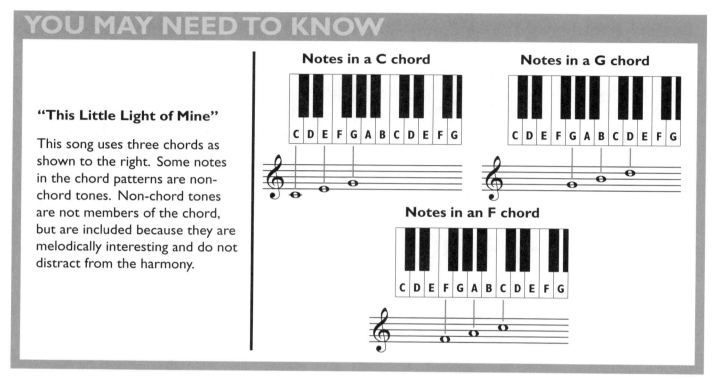

YOU MAY NEED TO KNOW

"This Little Light of Mine"

This song uses three chords as shown to the right. Some notes in the chord patterns are non-chord tones. Non-chord tones are not members of the chord, but are included because they are melodically interesting and do not distract from the harmony.

Notes in a C chord

Notes in a G chord

Notes in an F chord

This Little Light of Mine

📄 **Save the song.**

◼ Unit 2 Extensions and Supplemental Activities

Enrichment Activities

1. Create a new staff and compose a countermelody to "London Bridge" or "Jingle Bells."

2. Copy and paste accompaniment patterns from "Whole World" or "Little Light" into a new staff added to "London Bridge" or "Jingle Bells." Since the chords are not labeled in "London Bridge," you'll have to use your ear to determine which to use.

3. Create additional rhythmic patterns for the chords and harmonize any of the songs with those rhythmic patterns. As you create the various harmonies, try to create some which are better suited for general use, beginnings, endings, or transitions. Harmonize the songs with the new patterns but use the best-suited accompaniment for each part of the song.

4. Enter expressive markings such as crescendos and decrescendos into the pieces.

5. Add a *ritard* to the end of the pieces.

6. Use the *drum groove* or *rhythm-section generator* feature of your software (if available) to create a more complex accompaniment.

7. Convert "London Bridge" or "Jingle Bells" to a round. Does this work?

Web Extensions

1. Are there any other pieces that use excerpts of "Jingle Bells" or "London Bridge?"

2. Research historical information on "London Bridge." http://www.google.com

3. Research historical information on "Jingle Bells." http://www.google.com

4. Research historical information on "Whole World," and "Little Light." http://www.google.com

5. Take a short, familiar song from the web, open it with your notation program, and identify all measures which are the same. http://www.sibelius.com/ or http://www.makemusic.com/

Multimedia Extensions

Create a PowerPoint or Keynote presentation and include the following information:

1. Explain how repetition and contrast make a piece more interesting.

2. Explain what harmony adds to a piece of music.

3. Explain the background of the songs found in the Web-Extension activities above.

Computer-Assisted Instruction Extensions

MakingMusic (Morton Sobotnick, www.creatingmusic.com)

1. Drag animal-shaped building blocks to build a piece.

2. How is this like the "copy and paste" operation used in this unit?

Rock, Rap, 'n Roll: Drag building blocks into place to create a piece.

GarageBand: Drag building blocks into place to create a piece.

SmartMusic: A copy of the SmartMusic files for songs in this unit are found on the accompanying data CD, in the SmartMusic folder.

1. Load the song(s) into SmartMusic.

2. Sing or play along.

Keyboard Connection

1. Play "London Bridge," "Jingle Bells" and other melodies from this unit on the piano keyboard.

Sequencing Connections

1. Open the tune "He's Got the Whole World In His Hands" in your sequencer. Change timbres, add volume, add panning, and change tempo.

2. After completing step 1, record an accompanying drum part.

Composing Music with Notation

Composing a Song in a 16-Bar Form

■ Objectives

Upon completion of this unit, you will:

- Compose tonic and dominant melodies and harmonies.

- Compose a musical phrase with two different endings.

- Reconstruct songs in 16-bar form.

- Compose a song using 16-bar form.

- Enter notes and rhythms.

- Copy and paste phrases.

■ Activity 3.1 Listen to a 16-Bar Song Form

Songs are frequently composed in a 16-bar form. In this structure, the song contains four phrases of four measures each. The first, second, and last phrases are the same, except for their ending. The third phrase contains a contrasting melody.

The song, *Ode to Joy* (see below) is composed in 16-bar form. Notice the labels A, A1, B, A1. The **1** beside the A means that this phrase is the same as A, but with minor changes. In this case, A and A1 are the same except for the ending.

 1. Open the file <u>Unit03-01</u> and press play. An arrangement of *Ode to Joy* will play.

2. Can you identify the various sections (A, A1, B, and A1)?

3. Can you hear the difference between A and A1?

4. How are A and B different? _____

Ode to Joy

Beethoven

Open the file <u>Unit03-02</u>. This file has the accompaniment and chord symbols entered on a second staff.

1. Enter the notation for the melody on the top staff. Notice that phrases one, two, and four are nearly identical. Copy phrase one and paste it into phrases two and four to save time. Don't forget to change the last three notes of phrases two and four. When finished, the music will look like the example below.

2. Label the names of each section (A, A1, B, A1) using text.

3. Listen to the completed file. Does it sound correct?

A: Enter this melody first. Copy it.

A1: Paste the melody above here. Change the last three notes.

B: Enter this melody last.

A1: Paste the first melody from above here. Change the last three notes.

💾 **Save the song.**

Activity 3.3 Construct a 16-Bar Song

Open the file <u>Unit03-03</u>. This file contains building blocks for another 16-bar song.

1. Copy and paste the melody from phrase one into phrase two and four. Change the last three notes as indicated below.

2. Label the names of each section (A, A1, B, A1) using text.

3. Listen to the completed file. Does it sound correct?

16-Bar Song – Example 1

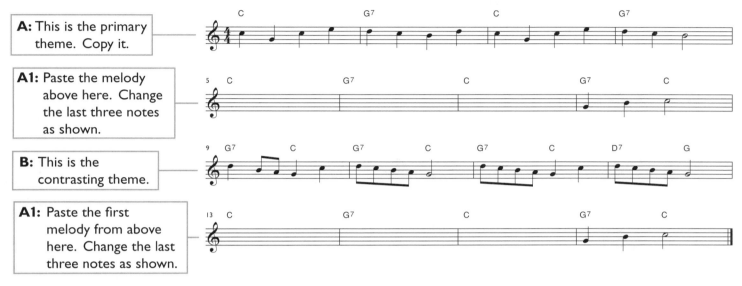

A: This is the primary theme. Copy it.

A1: Paste the melody above here. Change the last three notes as shown.

B: This is the contrasting theme.

A1: Paste the first melody from above here. Change the last three notes as shown.

 Save the song.

 Construct a Second 16-Bar Song

Open the file <u>Unit03-04</u>. This file contains building blocks for another 16-bar song.

1. Copy and paste the melody from phrase one into phrase two and four. Change the last three notes as indicated below.

2. Label the names of each section (A, A1, B, A1) using text.

3. Listen to the completed file. Does it sound correct?

16-Bar Song – Example 2

A: This is the primary theme. Copy it.

A1: Paste the melody above here. Change the last three notes as shown.

B: This is the contrasting theme.

A1: Paste the first melody from above here. Change the last three notes as shown.

 Save the song.

■ Activity 3.4 Build a 16-Bar Song from Smaller Building Blocks

Open the file <u>Unit03-05</u> This file contains building blocks for another 16-bar song. Using the building blocks below, create a 16-bar phrase.

1. Drag the building blocks for the A theme into the appropriate measures.

2. Match the chords of each building block to the chord shown in each measure of the song below.

3. Each A theme (phrases one, two, and four) should be the same except for the ending.

4. Some building blocks work best as endings. Others work best within the songs.

5. Drag the building blocks for the B theme into the appropriate measures (phrase three).

Build a 16-Bar Song

A Theme Building Blocks

B Theme Building Block

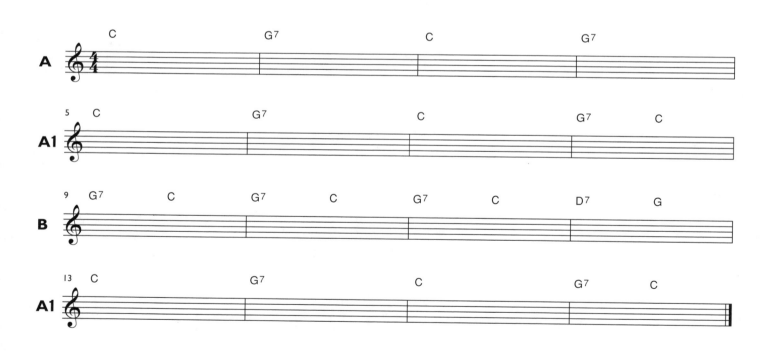

Save the song.

Activity 3.5 Compose a 16-Bar Song

 Open the file <u>Unit03-06</u> This file contains a template for an original 16-bar song.

1. Begin by composing melodies for each measure based on the chords and rhythms shown below.

2. The melodies may contain any note but, as a general rule, every other note should be one of those indicated below.

   a. C chord: C, E, and G.

   b. G^7 chord: G, B, D, and F.

   c. D^7 chord: D, F♯, A, and C.

   d. G chord: G, B, and D.

3. After composing the building blocks, copy them into the appropriate places in the song. Compose the building blocks and song below.

Build a 16-Bar Song

Step 1: Compose Building Blocks

Step 2: Create an Original 16-bar Form

 Save the song.

■ Unit 3 Extensions and Supplemental Activities

Enrichment Activities

1. Locate and enter the English and German lyrics for *Ode to Joy*.

2. Compose lyrics for the song.

3. Copy the block chords from *Ode to Joy* into a second staff in the new song. Arpeggiate them. Since the chords are the same, the harmony should work for either song.

4. Use the drum groove or rhythm-section generator to create an accompaniment to the composed song.

5. Add dynamic changes to the beginning of each phrase.

6. Put a *ritard* at the end.

 7. Analyze other songs in similar 16-bar form. Answer the following questions: Can you identify the various sections (A, A1, B, and A1)? Can you hear the difference between A and A1? How are A and B different?

    a. "Lightly Row": Open the file <u>Unit03-07</u>.

    b. Theme from *New World Symphony*: Open the file <u>Unit03-08</u>.

    c. "Mary Ann" (16 bars, but different form): Open the file <u>Unit03-09</u>.

 8. Open the file, *Ode to Joy* (file <u>Unit03-01</u>). Create a new staff above and copy and paste the melody composed in <u>Unit03-03</u> into the staff. If done correctly, the two melodies should be complimentary and produce a richer musical texture.

Web Extensions

On the companion CD, open the projects listed below.

1. The melody, *Ode To Joy*, was used by Beethoven in the fourth movement of his 9th Symphony. Navigate to http://www.lucare.com/immortal/audio.html and listen to the Lizst piano transcription of Beethoven's 9th Symphony, Movement 4. How is the melody similar to that used so far? How is it different?

2. Research information on the origin of this tune. http://www.google.com

3. Research information on Beethoven's 9th Symphony. http://www.google.com

4. Copy and paste the lyrics from the web into a word-processing document. http://www.niehs.nih.gov/kids/search.htm

5. Go to a sheet music site such as http://www.mysheetmusic.com. Print out a piece that you like and enter it in your notation program.

Multimedia Extensions

Create a PowerPoint or Keynote presentation and include the following information:

1. Define 16-bar form.

2. Explain how a 16-bar song is created.

3. Give background information on *Ode to Joy*.

4. Give background information on Beethoven's 9th Symphony, the *Choral Symphony*.

Computer-Assisted Instruction Extensions

Lessons from *Alfred's Essentials of Music Theory*, Book 3 (www.alfred.com)

1. Basic Forms of Music

SmartMusic practice activity. A copy of the SmartMusic files for *Ode to Joy*, "Lightly Row," "New World Symphony" and "Mary Ann" are found on the accompanying data CD, in the SmartMusic folder. For notation files, see <u>Unit03-07</u> to <u>Unit03-09</u>.

1. Load the song(s) into SmartMusic.

2. Sing or play along.

Keyboard Connection

1. Play the melodies "Ode to Joy" and "Lightly Row" on the piano keyboard.

Sequencing Connections

1. Print out the song you created in the "Compose a 16-Bar Song" section of this unit. Play and record it in your sequencer.

2. Add a drum track to the file created in step 1, above. Go to the loop browser and add drum loops.

Jazz Arranging (Dixieland, Swing, Partner Songs)

■ Objectives

In this lesson, several notation and musical skills will be mastered.

- Adding articulations including accent, tenuto, and staccato markings.

- Adding ties to create complex rhythms.

- Swinging eighth notes on playback.

- Creating additional staves.

- Entering a partner-song melody.

- Creating harmony for the 12-bar blues.

- Improvising a melody over the 12-bar blues.

- Making a melody more characteristic of a jazz style by adding swing rhythms and jazz articulations.

■ Jazz

Jazz is an American art form that mixes African-American influences with European traditions. Harmonically, jazz is much more interesting than European music. Most European harmony is based on a three-note chord. Most jazz harmony is based on a four- or five-note chord as indicated below.

Common European Harmony

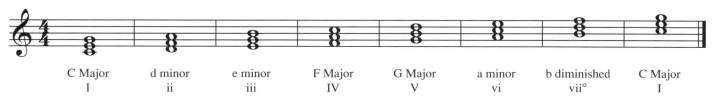

C Major	d minor	e minor	F Major	G Major	a minor	b diminished	C Major
I	ii	iii	IV	V	vi	vii°	I

Common Jazz Harmonies (seventh chord)

C7   dm7   em7   F7   G7   am7   b dim7   C7

Enter "Oh, When the Saints."

1. Create a score with a piano staff.

2. Enter the melody of "Oh, When the Saints" as shown below into the top staff.

3. Compose a harmony based on a variation of the given chords (see Units 2 and 3 for examples).

Oh, When The Saints

American Folk Tune

Oh,   when   the   saints———————— go   march - ing   in,————

— Oh,   when   the   saints   go   march -   ing   in,————

— Oh,   how   I   want   to   be   in   that   num - ber,————

—   when   the   saints   go   march -   ing   in.

■ **Additional Activities**

 Use the file created above, or open file Unit04-01.

1. Experiment with different dynamics.

2. Choose a tempo for this melody.

3. Add a staff and compose accompaniment patterns using the notes of the C, F and G chords (See page 40).

4. Choose different instruments for each staff.

 Save the song.

Entering "This Train is Bound for Glory":

1. Create a score with a piano staff.

2. Enter the melody of "This Train is Bound for Glory" as shown below into the top staff.

3. Compose a harmony based on a variation of the given chords (see Units 2 and 3 for examples).

This Train is Bound for Glory

American Folk Tune

This train_____ is bound for glo - ry, this train._____

This train_____ is bound for glo - ry, this train._____

This train_____ is bound for glo - ry, Don't ride none but the good and ho - ly,

This train_____ is bound for glo - ry, this train._____

■ Additional Activities

 Use the file created above or open file <u>Unit04-02</u>.

1. Experiment with different dynamics.

2. Choose a tempo for this melody.

3. Add a staff and compose accompaniment patterns using the notes of the C, F and G chords. NOTE: This song and the one on the previous page use the same chord progression. If you composed an accompaniment above, you can copy and paste it into this song.

4. Choose different instruments for each staff.

 Save the song.

■ Activity 4.3 Partner Songs

You may have noticed that the chord progressions for "Oh, When the Saints" and "This Train is Bound for Glory" are the same. When two melodies use the same harmonies, they can be played at the same time.

 1. Open "This Train is Bound for Glory" (Unit04-02a).

2. Copy the melody into the computer's clipboard.

 3. Open "Oh, When the Saints" (Unit04-01a).

4. Add a new staff above.

5. Paste the melody of "This Train is Bound for Glory" into the first full measure of the new staff so that the two melodies align as shown below.

6. Listen to the result.

Activity 4.4 Making a Song "Swing"

There are many different types of jazz. An early form was Dixieland. Open the file Unit04-04 and listen to it. The melody is "Oh, When the Saints" harmonized in a Dixieland style. Now, open the file Unit04-05 and listen to it. The melody is the same, but this time the tempo is slower and the style has a more mature sound. This style is known as "swing."

 1.   Open the file Unit04-06 and listen to it. This is also a swing style, but the rhythms are not performed correctly.

2.   Set the playback style to *swing* (consult your program's reference manual for specific instructions).

3.   Experiment with different tempos and swing settings.

4.   Open the Saved Partner Songs Activity. Set its playback style to swing.

Activity 4.5 Adding a Drum Part

 Open the file Unit04-06 and listen to it. The melody is "Oh, When the Saints" harmonized in a Dixieland style. Notice that the drums are a significant part of the arrangement.

1.   Open the file Unit04-07, it contains the melody of "Oh, When the Saints" and several drum building blocks which may be added to the song.

2.   Listen to the various drum-building blocks and drag them to the staff below the melody.

YOU MAY NEED TO KNOW

Percussion instruments are commonly mapped to the staff as follows:

1.   First space below the staff – closed hi-hat.

2.   First space in the staff – bass drum.

3.   Third space in the staff – snare drum.

4.   First space above the staff – ride cymbal.

Oh, When The Saints

American Folk Tune

Additional Activities

Create additional building blocks using percussion and use them to accompany the melody.

- Use your notation's rhythm-section generator (if available) to create an additional percussion accompaniment.

 Save the song.

Activity 4.6 Adding a Bass Part

Open the file Unit04-08. Add a bass part to "Oh, When the Saints."

1. Create a bass part that outlines the chords indicated below.
2. Use the notation program's rhythm-section generator (if available) to create a bass part (see below).

Oh, When The Saints

■ 12-Bar Blues: Harmony

One of the most common harmonic jazz progressions is the 12-bar blues. It is shown in the key of C below.

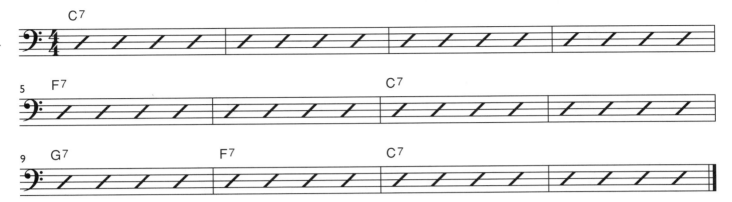

NOTE: This progression is repeated with melodies freely improvised. The last C7 is frequently played as G7 until the last verse.

■ Activity 4.7 Create a 12-Bar Blues Harmony

 Open the file Unit04-09.

1. At the top of the piece are building blocks which can be used to reconstruct the 12-bar blues harmony.

2. Use the copy and paste feature to move the building blocks to the correct measure.

Twelve-Bar Blues

Blues Building Blocks

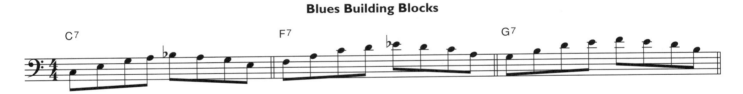

The Twelve-Bar Blues Progression

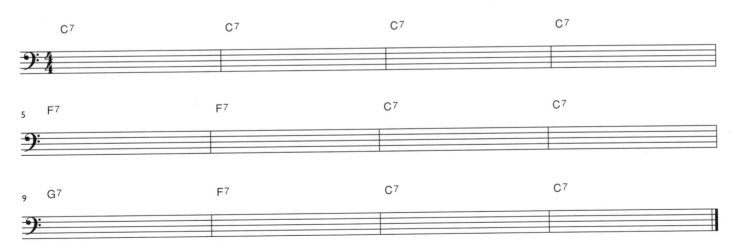

The melodies created when performing the blues are often based on the blues scale as shown below.

Blues Scale

 1. Open the file Unit04-10.

2. Using the notes of the blues scale and half-, quarter- and eighth-note values, compose a blues melody.

Twelve-Bar Blues

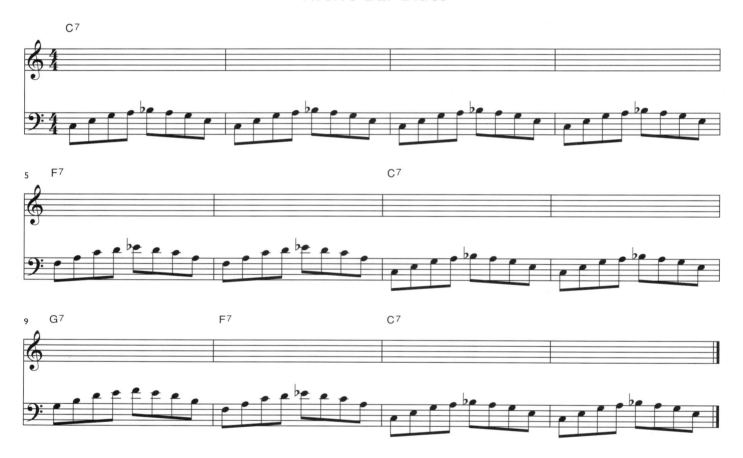

■ **Additional Activities**

1. Add a drum part.

2. Enter a tempo marking.

3. Enter dynamics and expressions.

Unit 4 Extensions and Supplemental Activities

Enrichment Activities

1. Create and enter lyrics for the twelve-bar blues piece composed.

2. Use the drum groove or rhythm-section generator to create an accompaniment to the composed 12-bar blues piece.

Web Extensions

1. Do a search on partner songs. http://www.google.com

2. Find MIDI files for partner songs.

3. Import the MIDI files into notation software and play them together.

4. Search on the web for information on jazz, Dixieland, blues, and swing.

5. Upload your piece to the showcase areas featured on the website of the manufacturer of the notation software (Finale/Sibelius).

6. Create a website with the 12-bar blues composed in this lesson. Include links so that the person viewing the site may do as many of the following as possible.

    a. Listen to a Standard MIDI File.

    b. View a Scorch version of the file.

    c. Download a Finale file and open it in Finale or Finale NotePad.

    d. Download a Sibelius version of the file and open it in Sibelius or Sibelius Demo.

7. Identify popular music which is based on the twelve-bar blues.

Multimedia Extensions

Create a PowerPoint or Keynote presentation and include the following information:

1. Define Jazz, Dixieland, Blues, Swing and give a brief history of each.

2. Explain twelve-bar blues harmony.

3. Describe the theory of the blues scale.

Computer-Assisted Instruction Extensions

Lessons from *Alfred's Essentials of Music Theory*, Book 3 (www.alfred.com)

1. 12-Bar Blues Chord Progression and Blues Scale

GarageBand, *Fruity Loops* or *Acid*.

1. Create a new song.

2. Select or construct a twelve-bar blues progression.

3. Record a melody based on the blues scale.

Rock, Rap, 'n Roll

1. Navigate to the blues section.

2. Construct a 12-bar blues progression from the building blocks in the program.

3. Create a melody to be performed over the progression using the building blocks in the program.

SmartMusic: A copy of the SmartMusic files for "Oh, When the Saints," and "This Train is Bound for Glory" can be found on the accompanying data CD, in the SmartMusic folder.

1. Load the song(s) into SmartMusic.

2. Sing or play along.

3. Finale uses: create a SmartMusic accompaniment for the 12-bar blues composed in this lesson. Load it and sing or play along.

Keyboard Connection

1. Play the 12-bar blues melody composed in this unit on the piano keyboard. Play the 12-bar blues progression in broken and block chords.

2. Play "Oh, When the Saints Go Marching In" and other songs with left-hand block chords and right-hand melody.

3. Play jazz cymbal patterns using percussion sounds.

4. Use pitch bend to perform melodies from this unit.

5. Improvise using patterns form the blues scale.

Sequencing Connections

1. Save the songs you created in this unit as standard MIDI files and open in your sequencer.

2. Add a drum track to the files created in step 1, above. Go the loop browser and add drum loops.

3. Play and record a jazz pattern using cymbal sounds.

■ Notes

Composing a Song in Theme and Variations Form

■ Objectives

In this lesson, several notation and musical skills will be introduced and practiced:

- Entering notes (variations).

- Transposing notes diatonically (modally).

- Changing the key signature (transposition).

- Creating a variation on an existing theme by:

    a. Adding a countermelody (descant or obligato).

    b. Using rhythmic variation.

    c. Using melodic variation.

    d. Applying a change of mode or key signature.

    e. Changing the texture of the piece.

■ Definition: Theme and Variations

Theme and Variations is a commonly-used classical technique for writing music in which an existing melody (theme) is played then repeated several times, but with changes (variations) each time.

Theme and Variations in Everyday Life

| **Chair** | **Rocking Chair 1** | **Rocking Chair 2** | **Papasan Chair** | **Bean Bag** |

Theme and Variations in Art

Van Gogh Sunflowers 1 **Van Gogh Sunflowers 2** **Van Gogh Sunflowers 3**

Activity 5.1 Listen to Theme and Variations: Melody with a Descant

Open the file <u>Unit05-01</u>. This is a recording of an excerpt from the second movement of Haydn's Symphony No. 94, known as the *Surprise Symphony*. This excerpt includes the theme and one variation.

- The first part of the song is the melody (theme).

- The second part of the song contains the variation. You can still hear the melody and may be able to hum along. This part, however, contains changes to the melody. What are the differences between the theme and the variation? _____

Symphony No. 94
(Theme from the *Surprise Symphony*)

F. J. Haydn

Variation 1, Melody with a Descant
Haydn's Symphony No. 94, 2nd Movement, excerpt

■ Activity 5.2 Create a Variation: Melody with a Descant

In the listening example on the previous page, the melody is the same in both the theme and variation sections. In the variation section, however, a countermelody, called a descant, is added.

 1.   Open the file Unit05-02.

2.   The melody of the song is found in staff two and a harmony part in staff three.

3.   The first staff contains a one-note descant melody. Your task is to improve the descant by moving the notes to different lines or spaces. Let your ear tell you where to place each note, but using notes from the chord usually works well.

 4.   Open file Unit05-03 and play it.

Move the notes on the top staff to compose a descant countermelody.

An example of a countermelody composed from the previous example is printed below.

 Save the song.

■ Activity 5.3 Listening to Theme and Variations: Rhythmic Variation

 1. Open the file <u>Unit05-04</u> This song also contains the theme and a variation from Haydn's Symphony No. 94.

2. Can you distinguish between the two sections (theme and variation)?

3. What are the differences between the theme and the variation? Study the melodies below for a hint.

■ Create a Variation: Rhythmic Variation

In the example above, the notes used in the melody and the variation are the same. In the variation, however, some notes are played with a different rhythm.

 1. Open the file <u>Unit05-05</u>.

2. The melody of the song is found in staff two.

3. Rewrite the melody in staff one using rhythms selected from those shown below. Compose your variation below.

 Save the song.

Twinkle, Twinkle

Alfred's Music Tech Series

■ Activity 5.4 Listening to Theme and Variations: Mode Variation

Open the file <u>Unit05-06</u>. This file contains the theme and another variation from Haydn's Symphony No. 94.

1. Can you distinguish between the two sections (theme and variation)?

2. What are the differences between the theme and the variation? Study the melodies below for a hint.

■ Create a Variation: Changing the melody to parallel minor

In the example above, the melody is in a major key and the variation is in a minor key. Melodies in major keys sound bright and higher, while those in a minor key sound dark and lower.

 1. Open the file <u>Unit05-07</u>.

2. Change the key signature of the song to three flats. Be sure to tell the software NOT to transpose the notes (keep or hold them on their original lines or spaces).

3. If you've done this correctly, the theme will look very similar to the original but with a different key signature. The sound on playback, however, will be quite different.

4. All Bs are flat because of the key signature. In minor songs, it is common to raise that note a half step, in this case by applying a natural sign. Change all B flats to B naturals.

 Save the song.

■ Studying Theme and Variations

You can learn about Theme and Variations by studying examples. Haydn's Symphony No. 94 contains numerous variation techniques. Below is a condensed version of each. Study each example and answer the questions below them.

Theme of Haydn's Symphony No. 94

Listen to <u>Unit05-08</u> to hear the theme of Haydn's Symphony No. 94, as shown above. You'll want to be well acquainted with this melody since each variation will be related to it.

1. Does this theme remind you of any other songs? *(Circle your answer)*   YES   NO

2. If so, what and why? _____

■ Variation 1 of Haydn's Symphony No. 94

Melody with a Descant

Variation 1 - Add an obligato part

Listen to <u>Unit05-09</u>, Variation 1 from Haydn's Symphony No. 94. This is the same theme as in example <u>Unit05-02</u>, but by studying it, we can learn more about writing variations. This variation uses a descant to create the variation.

1. When composers compose melodies, they use a combination of steps (moving from one note of the scale to the next, for example, A to B then B to C) and leaps (skipping over notes of the scale). The theme primarily uses leaps. Does the variation use primarily leaps or steps? _____

2. The rhythm of the theme is mostly eighth notes. What notes are most used in the variation? _____

3. Is the theme written in two-measure fragments? What about the variation? _____

4. How do the beginnings and ends of the theme and the descant align with one another? _____

5. The original theme is found in this variation. Does the presence of the descant make it harder to hear the theme? _____

Alfred's Music Tech Series

Melody with a Mode Change

Listen to <u>Unit05-10</u> to hear Variation 2 from Haydn's Symphony No. 94. This is the same theme as in example <u>Unit05-03</u>. This variation results from a change of mode from major to minor.

1. Is the only variation the change of the melody from major to minor? _____

2. Explain: _____

_____

_____

_____

■ Variation 3 of Haydn's Symphony No. 94

Rhythmic Variation

Variation 3 - Rhyhtmic Variation of Melody

Listen to Unit05-11, Variation 3 from Haydn's Symphony No. 94. This is the same theme as in example Unit05-01. This variation results from the application of a different rhythm to the notes of the theme.

1. Other than substituting sixteenth notes for the eighth notes, does Haydn use any other variation techniques? _____ If so, what? _____

2. Is it easy to hear the theme within this variation? _____

3. Is it easier to hear the theme in this variation than the ones above? _____

■ Variation 4 of Haydn's Symphony No. 94

Addition of Two Descants

Variation 4 - Addition of two obligato parts

Listen to Unit05-12, Variation 4 from Haydn's Symphony No. 94.

1. What variation techniques does Haydn use? _____

2. This variation also includes the original theme. Is it easy to hear the theme in this variation?

    (Circle your answer)   YES   NO   Why or why not? _____

    _____

    _____

■ Variation 5 of Haydn's Symphony No. 94

Descant with Altered Theme Embedded

Variation 5 - Addition of another obligato part containing melodic variation of theme

Listen to Unit05-13, Variation 5 from Haydn's Symphony No. 94.

1. In this variation (top staff), Haydn includes virtually every note of the melody but mixes them with ornamental notes. Circle the notes of the theme in the top staff.

2. Does Haydn place the notes of the melody in the same place in the beat each time, or does he move them around? _____

■ Variation 6 of Haydn's Symphony No. 94

Melodic Variation and Rhythmic Accompaniment

Variation 6 - Melodic embellishment and rhythmic accompaniment

Listen to Unit05-14, Variation 6 from Haydn's Symphony No. 94.

1. Are the notes from the melody found within the variation in measure one and two?

   (Circle your answer)   YES   NO   If yes, mark the notes.

2. How are measures 2 and 3 of the variation and the original melody the same? _____

   _____

   How are they different? _____

   _____

3. What does the accompaniment do in measures 1 and 2, and 5 and 6 that is different? _____

   _____

   _____

■ Variation 7 of Haydn's Symphony No. 94

Descant with Melodic and Harmonic Variation

Variation 7 - Addition of another obligato part

Listen to Unit05-15, Variation 7 from Haydn's Symphony No. 94.

1. Compare the rhythm of staff two with the rhythm of the original theme. Is it the same or different? Explain. _____

2. Compare the notes of staff two with the notes of the original theme. Are they the same or different? Explain. _____

3. Compare the top staff of the variation with the second staff. Are the notes, rhythms, contour, and phrase lengths the same or different? _____
_____

■ Variation 8 of Haydn's Symphony No. 94

Theme with Harmonic Variation, Rhythmic Accompaniment, and Coda

Variation 8 - Ends song with altered harmony, melody, and rhythm

Listen to <u>Unit05-16</u>, Variation 8 from Haydn's Symphony No. 94.

1. The original theme is found in the middle staff, but this is still a variation. Does the variation result from a different melody, rhythm, or harmony? _____

    Explain: _____

    _____

2. The last four measures are designed to end the piece. They are based loosely on the melody.

    How? _____

Listening to a Variation of Meter and Tempo

A commonly used variation technique is to change the time signature or meter, and tempo of a piece.

1. Listen to each of the versions of "Twinkle, Twinkle, Little Star" below. (<u>Unit05-17</u>, <u>Unit05-18</u>, and <u>Unit05-19</u>).

2. Count to three, four, or five (matching the time signatures) out loud while listening to each measure of each piece below.

3. Note that the tempo of the $\frac{5}{4}$ variation is faster than the others.

Enter the version in $\frac{5}{4}$ into the notation program and print it.

1. Open a new file.

2. Create a piano part in $\frac{5}{4}$ time, key of C.

3. Enter the notation for the $\frac{5}{4}$ version below

Twinkle, Twinkle

Twinkle, Twinkle

Twinkle, Twinkle

■ Listen to a Variation

Open file <u>Unit05-20</u> and listen to it (Note: this file will play in a program such as Windows Media Player, iTunes, or something similar). This is a theme and variation version of the well-known melody, "Amazing Grace." This version contains variations on the melody, rhythm, and harmony. One of the most noticeable variations is a tempo change. Describe each variation below:

_____

_____

_____

■ Write a Variation

Below is the theme of "Amazing Grace." Compose two variations in the space provided. Use any of the techniques described in this unit or invent your own. Be creative! This can be entered into the software in the file <u>Unit05-20</u>.

Amazing Grace

Enrichment Activities

1. Using the activity file of "Amazing Grace" from the previous page, modify the rhythm of the harmony.

2. Using the activity file of "Amazing Grace" from the previous page, modify the harmony (add sharps or flats to chords just before a chord change).

3. Compose an original theme of sixteen measures. Write a variation on it.

Web Extensions

On the companion data CD, open the projects listed below.

1. Listen to a MIDI file of the Mozart's "Twinkle Variations" (Unit05-22).

    a. Is the theme the same melody that you know?

    b. What variation techniques can you identify?

    c. Do any of the variations use the techniques described in this unit?

    d. Do any of the variations use techniques not found in this unit? Explain.

2. Research information on theme and variation form.

    a. Describe the use of this form by famous composers.

    b. Describe the use of this form in popular music.

    c. Identify additional variation techniques.

3. List other songs that are composed in theme and variation form.

4. Find the lyrics to "Amazing Grace" on the web. Add them to the score. Can you sing these words to other tunes ("I'd Like to Teach the World to Sing," "The House of the Rising Sun," etc.)?

5. Find the lyrics to "Twinkle, Twinkle Little Star" on the web. Add them to the score. Locate other lyrics which can be sung using this tune (ABC Song, "Baa, Baa, Black Sheep"). You may try a search on the words, "to the tune of twinkle" Use the quotes in the search.

6. Using the variations that you composed in this unit, save as a web page using Sibelius *Scorch*.

Multimedia Extensions

Create a PowerPoint or Keynote presentation with the following information:

1. Define theme and variations.

2. Summarize the variation techniques used in this unit.

3. Summarize other variation techniques found in the web searches above.

4. Include background information on Haydn's Symphony No. 94

5. Include background information on Mozart's "Twinkle Variations."

6. Make a list of songs in theme and variation form.

Computer-Assisted Instruction Extensions

Lessons from *Alfred's Essentials of Music Theory*, Book 3 (www.alfred.com)

1. Basic Forms of Music

SmartMusic: A copy of the SmartMusic files for Haydn's Symphony No. 94, "Twinkle, Twinkle Little Star," and "Amazing Grace" are found on the accompanying data CD.

1. Load the song(s) into SmartMusic.

2. Sing or play along.

Keyboard Connections

1. Play some, or all, of the variations you created, on the piano keyboard.

Sequencing Connections

1. Save the songs you created in this unit as standard MIDI files and open in your sequencer.

2. Add a drum track to the files created in step 1, above. Go the loop browser and add drum loops.

Conclusion

The goals of this book are to broaden your understanding of music and introduce you to composing through the use of notation software. Hopefully, as a result of your study, you are better able to understand, respond to, enjoy, and create music.

As a reader of musical notation, you now have access to an extensive library of compositions from the best musical minds in the world. Your enjoyment is just beginning. You may want to stop by the library or your local music store to see what else is available.

As a composer, you have the potential to leave a musical legacy for generations to come. To rise to this level, however, you will need to (1) practice your existing skills, (2) continue to learn more about music, and (3) find inspiration that gives you a unique musical voice.

Practicing existing skills will be important. Like many skills, if you are not actively using them, you will begin to lose them. It's time to think about what is next, and to take on additional projects that will allow you to grow. Will you compose a new solo for your primary instrument, write for an ensemble of your friends, or create the next top-40 hit? Anything is possible, but these things will only happen as you discipline yourself to work and improve.

The best way to learn more about music is to listen to and study it. When listening, don't limit yourself to one or a few styles. There are numerous highly developed kinds of music with much to offer. The master composer knows and understands many styles. When you hear something you like, find the notation to see how it is done. When you understand it, you will be able to add those techniques to your musical vocabulary.

Inspiration is often said to be that element that separates good music from great. Each composer will seek and find his or her own inspiration, but those whose music reflects the things that resonate with his or her peers and the public will find the greatest success.

In all of these tasks, notation software is a powerful tool that enables you to be effective and efficient. With it, you can explore and experiment, copy and paste for repetition, transpose and modify for variety, and automate many compositional processes. The ideas will be your own, but the tool will make you faster and, hopefully, better.

The authors of this series wish you the best in your music making. We trust that you will find it to be a lifetime undertaking that is both rich and rewarding.

Floyd Richmond

Tom Rudolph

Lee Whitmore

Stefani Langol

■ Fundamentals and Rules of Music Notation

This section provides an overview of the fundamentals of music and rules of notation. Those who have limited experience working with music notation should read through this chapter, preferably with the help of a teacher, and refer to it when they have questions.

■ A Basic Role of Notation

Which note should I play?

The modern piano has 88 keys. Electronic instruments may have as many as 120. One of the most basic functions of notation is to tell the performer which note to play.

Piano with 88 keys

Electronic instrument or software screen with 120 notes

A number of musical symbols are used to indicate which note is to be played. The most fundamental symbol is the staff, a set of five lines.

Staff

Another fundamental symbol is that of a note, which represents a single sound or pitch. For now, we'll begin with the simplest of note shapes, an unfilled circle, also known as a whole note.

Whole Note

Each note of the piano, or any instrument, is indicated by a note in a specific location on a staff. As a general principle, low notes on the keyboard are located on the left and high notes on the right.

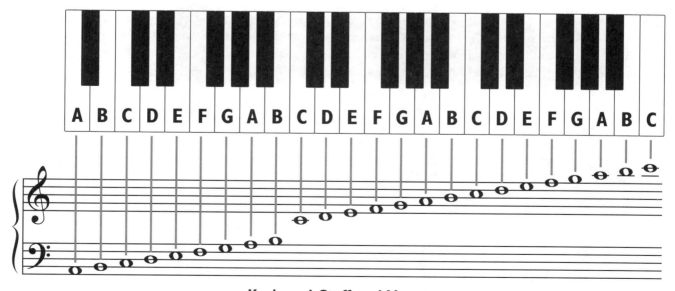

Keyboard, Staff, and Notes

As shown on the previous page, it takes two staves to show the notes that are used most often on the piano. Piano players usually play the higher notes (in the top staff) with their right hand and the lower notes (in the lower staff) with their left. **Clef signs**, as shown below, are used to indicate which staff is being used and the position of notes within the staff.

Treble or G-clef symbol
This clef shows the position of G.

Bass or F-clef symbol
This clef shows the position of F.

When the staves are used together, as shown above, they are called the **grand staff.**

Grand Staff

When notes outside the staff are needed, **ledger lines** are used. **Ledger lines** are small lines above or below the staff to show the position of high or low notes. You may use as many ledger lines as needed.

A high note　　　　　　　　　　　　**A low note**

Most performers, however, don't like more than two or three ledger lines on a staff. The more ledger lines used, the easier it is to lose one's place. A common way to write high and low notes without using ledger lines is to write them in the staff and to indicate that they are to be transposed eight notes higher or lower. This distance of eight notes is an octave and is abbreviated *8va* or *8vb* as indicated below.

■ Note Names

Notes are named using the first seven letters of the alphabet. After G (the seventh note), the alphabet starts over. The distance from one A on the staff to the next A is an octave. It is one octave from any note to the next with the same name.

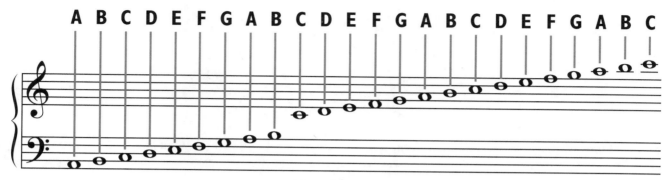

Note Names

Treble (G) Clef Notes: Some people like to memorize the names of all notes on the treble (G) clef staff lines using a saying such as Every Good Boy Does Fine, or all of the notes on the spaces using the word, FACE.

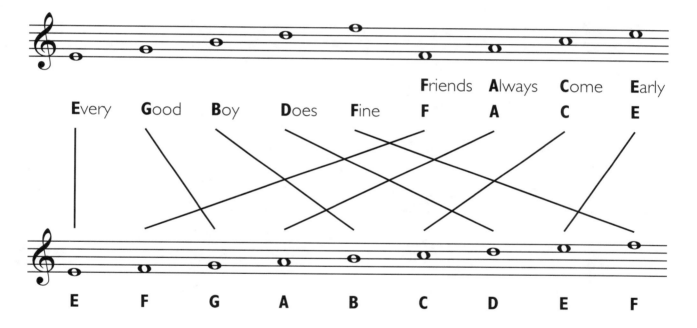

This system is helpful for quickly identifying note names, but it is just as easy, and perhaps more intuitive, to remember the alphabetical arrangement of the notes. Most music moves step wise up and down from one note to the next. As long as the student knows the note on which they start, it is easy to keep the letter names in mind. A tip for students is to practice saying the letter names alphabetically up and down, since music goes down as frequently as up.

Bass (F) Clef Notes: Again, many like to use sayings such as Great Big Dogs Fight Always and All Cows Eat Grass to help remember the note names. As before, this is a useful system but many students will find it easier just to use the alphabetic names.

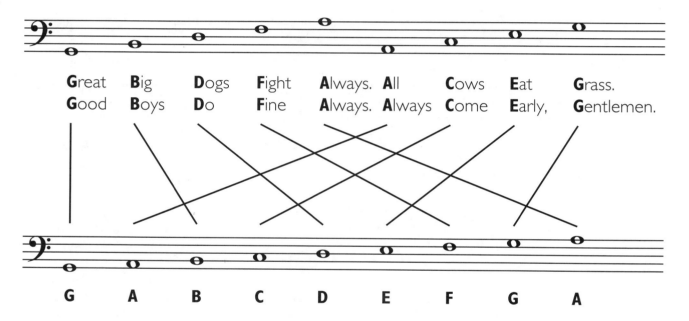

Alfred's Music Tech Series

■ Accidentals

In music, **accidentals** are used to indicate that the black notes of the keyboard should be used. The two most common accidentals are sharps and flats.

Sharp Sign   **Flat Sign**

A sharp sign indicates that one note higher than the original is desired. For example, see C and C♯ below. A flat sign indicates that one note lower than the original is desired. For example, see D and D♭ below. Notice that all black notes have more than one name. For example, C♯ and D♭ are the same note. These notes are said to be **enharmonic equivalents**. Also notice that some white keys don't have a black note between them. As a result, applying a sharp or flat to some notes results in a white key being played. (C♭, B♯, F♭, E♯)

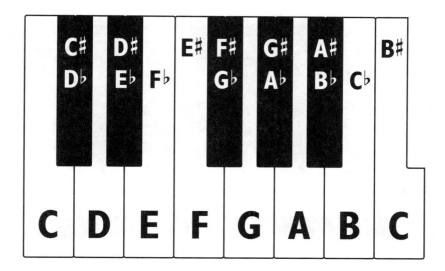

A third type of accidental is the natural sign. A natural sign cancels the effect of a sharp or flat and always produces a white note. In fact, the white notes of the keyboard may be identified by their short names (A, B, C, etc.), or by their long names (A natural, B natural, C natural, etc.).

Natural Sign

All accidentals are drawn to the left of the note to which they apply, but they are all pronounced after the note name. Note in the example below the position of the accidental and the names of the notes.

C   C Sharp   D   D Flat

Key Signatures

It has become common practice to write a **key signature** at the beginning of a piece of music that will identify the notes that will be sharp or flat for the entire song. There are fifteen possible major keys as shown below. As students write and perform music, they will become acquainted with most of these.

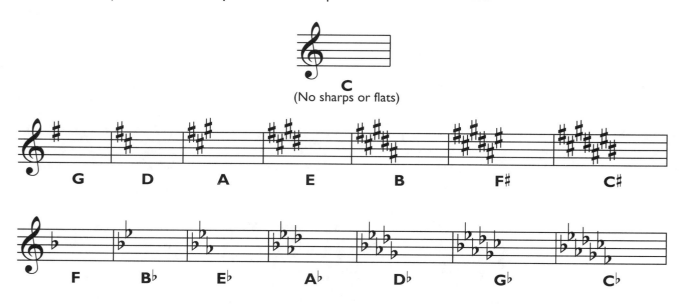

Sharps and flats that occur in the key signature last for the entire song, but it is possible for accidentals within the song to override the key signature.

By contrast, accidentals that occur within a piece only last to the end of the measure where they occur, and then, only if not overridden by another accidental. (See the rhythm section for an explanation of measures.)

Rhythm

In addition to telling the performer which note to play, the music must also tell when to start and stop. This is done by the shape of the note head, stem, and flag (or beam). Commonly used shapes are shown below.

The following chart shows the duration of the most common notes in the most used time signatures.

Note Shape	Name	Duration
𝅝	Whole Notes	4 beats each
𝅗𝅥	Half Notes	2 beats each
𝅘𝅥	Quarter Notes	1 beat each
Written in groups: 𝅘𝅥𝅮 Written individually: ♪	Eighth Notes	½ beat each
Written in groups: 𝅘𝅥𝅯 Written individually: ♬	Sixteenth Notes	¼ beat each
Written in groups: 𝅘𝅥𝅮 (3) Written individually: ♪ (3)	Triplets	⅓ beat each

When a note has a stem, the direction of the stem (up or down) is determined by the position of the note on the staff. When notes are on the middle line, the stems may go either way, although they are not usually mixed as in the chart above. When notes are above the middle line, the stems are drawn down (so they won't extend too far above the staff). When notes are below the middle line, the stems are drawn up (so they won't extend too far below the staff). When notes are beamed in groups, the stem direction is determined by the position of most of the notes. Stems that are drawn up are always on the right side of the note. Stems that are drawn down are always on the left.

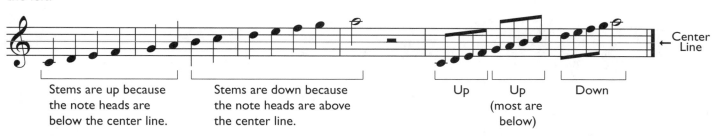

Stems are up because the note heads are below the center line.

Stems are down because the note heads are above the center line.

Up   Up (most are below)   Down   ← Center Line

■ Rhythmic Relationships

Notes

Rhythmic values are frequently twice as long or short as the next note value. This is illustrated in the chart below.

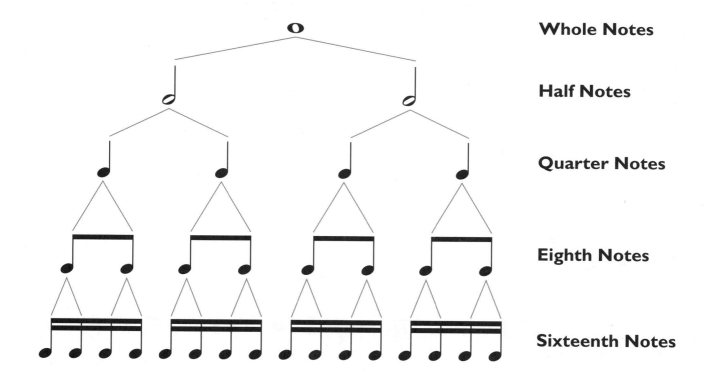

Whole Notes

Half Notes

Quarter Notes

Eighth Notes

Sixteenth Notes

Rests

Performing the correct notes at the correct time is essential for a good musical performance. Equally important is not performing at the incorrect time. When performers are to remain silent, it is indicated in their parts with rests. The relationships of the various rests are illustrated below.

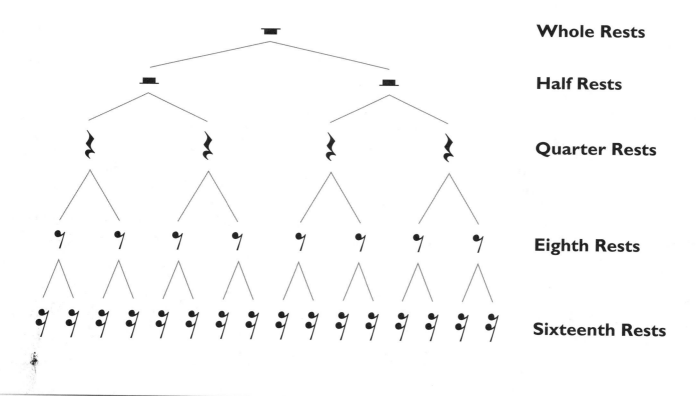

Whole Rests

Half Rests

Quarter Rests

Eighth Rests

Sixteenth Rests

Alfred's Music Tech Series

Patterns and Counting

Although the notes on the previous page can be assembled into any order (and frequently are by untrained musicians), there are a number of rhythmic patterns which are used more frequently. Of course, as the level of the music advances, the number of exceptions to this rule increases. Still, beginning musicians would do well to learn to write and perform the following patterns. Familiar ways of *counting* each of the patterns are found below.

Note	Name	Kodály	Gordon	Traditional
𝅝	Whole Note	Ta-ah-ah-ah	Du - - -	1-(2)-(3)-(4)
𝅗𝅥	Half Note	Ta-ah	Du -	1-(2)
𝅘𝅥	Quarter Note	Ta	Du	1
𝅘𝅥𝅮𝅘𝅥𝅮	Eighth Notes	Ti-ti	Du-de	1 &
𝅘𝅥𝅯𝅘𝅥𝅯𝅘𝅥𝅯𝅘𝅥𝅯	Sixteenth Notes	Ti-ka-ti-ka	Du-ta-de-ta	1 e & a
Triplet	Triplet	Trip-le-ti	Du-da-di	1-la-li *or* tri-ple-let
One-Beat Pattern	One-Beat Pattern	Ti-ti-ka	Du-de-ta	1 & a
One-Beat Pattern	One-Beat Pattern	Ti-ka-ti	Du-ta-de	1 e &
One-Beat Pattern	One-Beat Pattern	Syn-co-pah	Du-ta-ta	1 e (&) a
One-Beat Pattern	One-Beat Pattern	Trip-ka	Du--ta	1 (e) (&) a
Two-Beat Pattern	Two-Beat Pattern	Syn-co-pah	Du-de-de	1 & (2) &
Two-Beat Pattern	Two-Beat Pattern	Ta-i-ti	Du--de	1 (2) &

■ Meter and Time Signatures

Most music is rhythmically organized so the first of every two, three or four beats is accented. For that reason, many dance steps and movements repeat or change every few beats. *Meter* is the rhythmic grouping of notes into repeating patterns. When a song contains a pattern that is four beats long, we say that the music is in quadruple meter; when three, triple; and when two, duple.

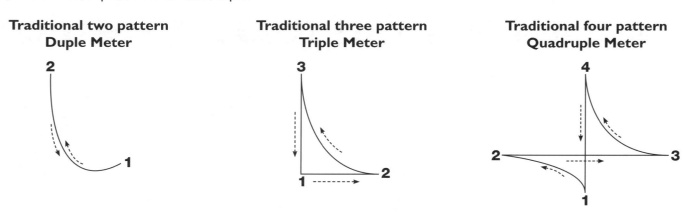

Traditional two pattern
Duple Meter

Traditional three pattern
Triple Meter

Traditional four pattern
Quadruple Meter

Conductors also move to the music in a way that reflects the meter. Sing through these songs while conducting a matching pattern below. Duple: "Yankee Doodle" Triple: "My Country 'Tis of Thee" Quadruple: "Are You Sleeping?" Recordings of these songs are available on the accompanying CD. You may want to practice the conducting patterns before trying to sing with them. NOTE: All of these songs begin on the accented beat (beat one). Start conducting at beat one on the underlined syllable above, then follow the lines to every beat in rhythm as marked.

At the beginning of the piece below are the numbers $\frac{4}{4}$. This is called the time signature. The top number of the time signature indicates the meter of the piece. The bottom number tells which kind of note gets one beat (See the next page for more information about time signatures). The most common quadruple meter is $\frac{4}{4}$, triple is $\frac{3}{4}$, and duple is $\frac{2}{4}$. After every four beats (below) there are vertical lines on the staff called bar lines. These divide the music into measures.

Are You Sleeping?

French Folk Tune

■ Pickup Notes

Many songs begin with an incomplete measure. The notes in the incomplete measure are commonly called pickup notes. The following songs, for instance, have a word or syllable before their accented beat. Duple: "When Johnny Comes Marching Home" Triple: "Amazing Grace" Quadruple: "Swing Low." Recordings of these songs are available on the accompanying CD. Sing through these songs while conducting a matching pattern above. Start conducting at beat one on the underlined syllable above, and then follow the lines to every beat in rhythm as marked. Again, you may want to practice the conducting patterns before trying to sing with them.

Amazing Grace

A - maz - ing— grace, how sweet the sound, that saved a— wretch like me.———— I

once——— was— lost, but now——— am— found, was blind but now I see.

It is a standard notational practice that when a song begins with an incomplete measure (pickup notes), the last measure contains the number of beats required to complete the first measure. This practice may seem odd, but it makes it possible to sing the song repeatedly while maintaining the correct number of beats in each measure.

■ More About Time Signatures

The most commonly used time signature is $\frac{4}{4}$. Consequently, it is often called **common time**. In fact, $\frac{4}{4}$ is so common that instead of putting $\frac{4}{4}$, many composers just draw a **C** instead.

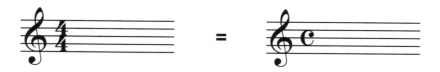

The bottom number of the time signature is frequently, but not always 4. There are two other commonly used bottom numbers for time signatures: 2 and 8. When there is a 2 on the bottom, the tempo of the piece moves twice as fast. When there is an 8 on the bottom, the tempo moves twice as slow. The following chart shows the value of notes for the various time signatures.

		Duration		
		Time signatures with a 2 on the bottom $\frac{2}{2}$ $\frac{3}{2}$	Time signatures with a 4 on the bottom $\frac{2}{4}$ $\frac{3}{4}$ $\frac{4}{4}$	Time signatures with an 8 on the bottom $\frac{3}{8}$ $\frac{6}{8}$ $\frac{9}{8}$
Note	**Name**			
𝅝	Whole Notes	2 beats each	4 beats each	8 beats each
𝅗𝅥	Half Notes	1 beat each	2 beats each	4 beats each
𝅘𝅥	Quarter Notes	½ beat each	1 beats each	2 beats each
♫	Eighth Notes	¼ beat each	½ beat each	1 beat each
♬	Sixteenth Notes	⅛ beat each	¼ beat each	½ beat each

The most observable effect of changing the bottom number of the time signature is to speed up or slow down the tempo by twice as much. Please note on the chart on the previous page that the note which gets one beat changes. Many people use this to help them remember the rhythmic values of the new time signature.

Time signatures with a 2 on the bottom	$\frac{2}{2}$ $\frac{3}{2}$	$\frac{1}{2}$ note gets a beat
Time signatures with a 4 on the bottom	$\frac{2}{4}$ $\frac{3}{4}$ $\frac{4}{4}$	$\frac{1}{4}$ note gets a beat
Time signatures with an 8 on the bottom	$\frac{3}{8}$ $\frac{6}{8}$ $\frac{9}{8}$	$\frac{1}{8}$ note gets a beat

■ Compound Time Signatures

One unique thing that happens with time signatures with an eight on the bottom (for example $\frac{3}{8}$, $\frac{6}{8}$, $\frac{9}{8}$, and $\frac{12}{8}$), is that they are frequently performed three times faster. Because there are, in effect, three eighth notes in every beat, music written in $\frac{3}{8}$ feels as though it has one beat per measure; music in $\frac{6}{8}$ feels as though it has two (duple meter); music in $\frac{9}{8}$ feels as though it has three (triple meter); and music in $\frac{12}{8}$ feels as though it has four (quadruple meter). Because each beat is subdivided into three parts, the meter is said to be **compound**.

■ Ties

From time to time, a composer desires to write long notes in places which would not normally be possible. By using ties (a small curved line connecting two notes), it is possible to do this. In the example below, the performer would play one note, but hold it for the duration of both. Ties frequently connect notes from one measure to the next, but they may be used within a measure as well. Ties always connect notes of the same name (C to C). Can you find the tied notes in the song, "Amazing Grace," on the previous page? Remember, look for two notes with the same name which are connected with a curved line.

■ Slurs

When composers want a passage to be played as smoothly as possible, with no rest or break between notes, they use **slurs**. Slurs are similar in appearance to ties, but they function differently. Slurs connect two different notes which are to be played smoothly, while ties connect two of the same notes which are to be played as one. Both slurs and ties may be used over a bar line as shown in the example below, or within a measure. Can you find the slurs in the song, "Amazing Grace"? Remember, look for two different notes connected with a curved line.

■ Dotted-Note Values

From time to time, a composer desires to write notes which are longer than the symbols discussed up to this point. By adding a **dot** to a note, the composer indicates to the performer that they should hold the note longer. The exact amount of additional time depends on the given note. For those who understand fractions, the amount of extra time is exactly one half the duration of the existing note. Thus a whole note which normally gets 4 beats (in time signatures with a 4 on the bottom) would get that amount (4 beats) plus half as much (2 beats) for a total of 6 beats (4+2=6). The chart below summarizes the values of the most common dotted notes.

Note	Name	Duration		
		Time signatures with a 2 on the bottom $\frac{2}{2}$ $\frac{3}{2}$	Time signatures with a 4 on the bottom $\frac{2}{4}$ $\frac{3}{4}$ $\frac{4}{4}$	Time signatures with an 8 on the bottom $\frac{3}{8}$ $\frac{6}{8}$ $\frac{9}{8}$
𝅝.	Dotted Whole Notes	3 beats each	6 beats each	12 beats each
𝅗𝅥.	Dotted Half Notes	1½ beats each	3 beats each	6 beats each
♩.	Dotted Quarter Notes	¾ beat each	1½ beats each	3 beats each
♪.	Dotted Eighth Notes	⅜ beat each	¾ beat each	1½ beats each
𝅘𝅥𝅯.	Dotted Sixteenth Notes	3/16 beat each	⅜ beat each	¾ beat each

NOTE: Dotted notes are almost always used with a partner note which completes the beat. For example, a dotted quarter note (1½ beats in $\frac{4}{4}$) is almost always used with an eighth note (½ beat in $\frac{4}{4}$). This combination of notes produces an even 2 beats in $\frac{4}{4}$.

Likewise, a dotted eighth note (¾ beats in $\frac{4}{4}$) is almost always used with a sixteenth note (¼ beat in $\frac{4}{4}$). This combination of notes produces 1 beat in $\frac{4}{4}$.

Can you find the dotted notes in the song, "Amazing Grace"? Are they partnered with notes which complete the beat?

■ Learn More

A number of instructional software programs teach the concepts in this unit. For more information, try the following programs: *Music Ace* I and II, or *Alfred's Essentials of Music Theory*.

■ Extensions and Supplemental Activities

Computer-Assisted Instruction Extensions

Lessons from *Music Ace* I

1. Lesson 1: Introduction to the Staff
2. Lesson 3: Playing with Pitch
3. Lesson 6: The ABC's of the Staff
4. Lesson 7: The ABC's of the Treble Staff
5. Lesson 8: More Treble Staff ABC's
6. Lesson 20: Sharps and Flats
7. Lesson 21: Sharps and Flats on the Staff
8. Lesson 22: More Sharps and Flats on the Staff
9. Lesson 23: The Key Signature

Lessons from *Music Ace* II

1. Lesson 3: Review 1: Note Names
2. Lesson 5: Basic Rhythm Notation
3. Lesson 9: The Measure
4. Lesson 11: Notes Longer than a Beat
5. Lesson 21: The Time Signature

Lessons from *Alfred's Essentials of Music Theory*, Book I

1. Staff, Notes and Pitches
2. Treble and Bass Clefs
3. Grand Staff and Ledger Lines
4. Note Values
5. Measure, Bar Line and Double Bar Line
6. $\frac{2}{4}$, $\frac{3}{4}$ and $\frac{4}{4}$ Time Signatures
7. Whole, Half and Quarter Notes and Rests
8. Ties and Slurs
9. Eighth Notes and Rests
10. Flats, Sharps, and Naturals

Lessons from *Alfred's Essentials of Music Theory*, Book II

1. Key Signatures
2. Pick-up Notes and Syncopation